At the Hospital

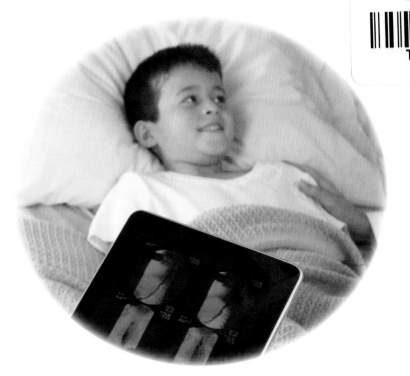

Written by Catherine Baker

Collins

2

5

6

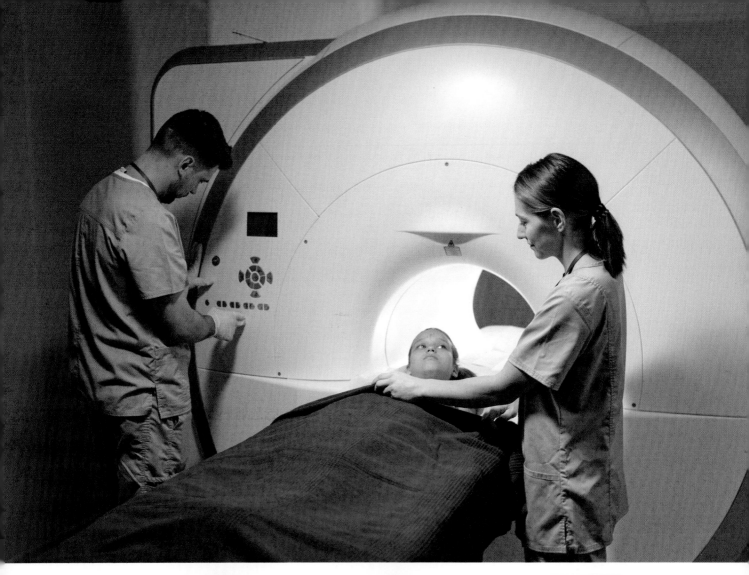

8

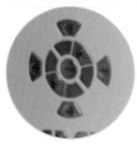

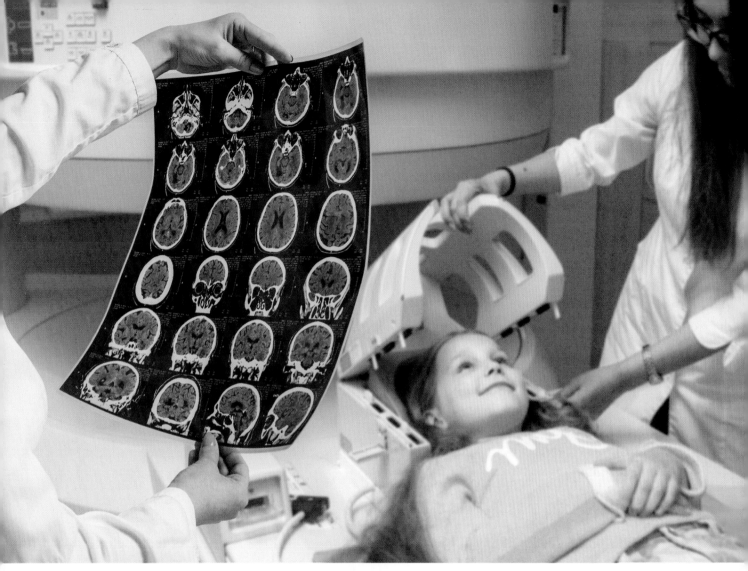

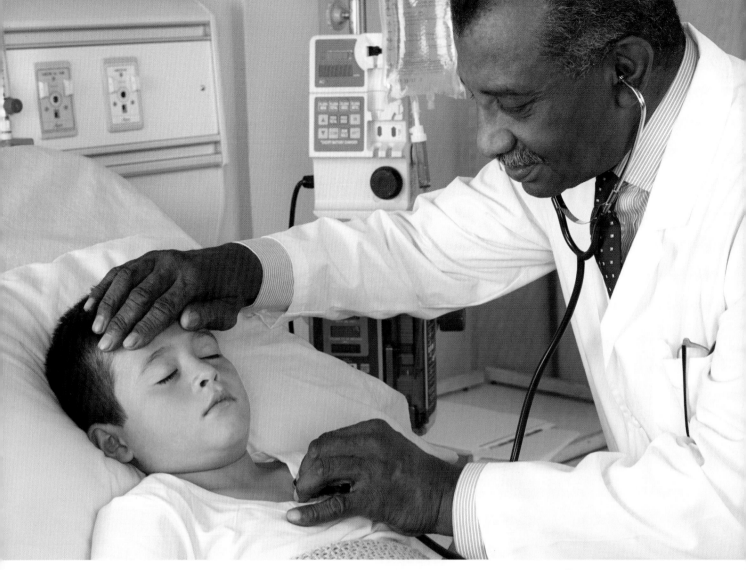

10

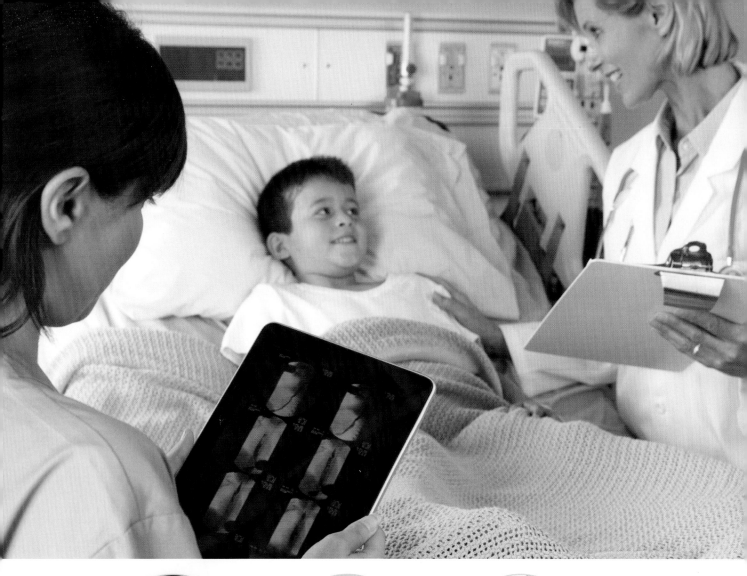

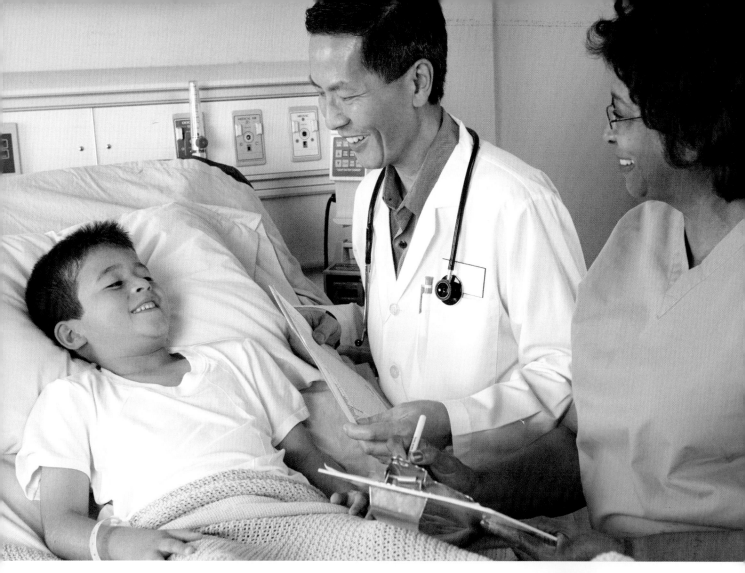

12

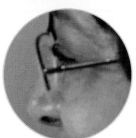

What's happening in each picture?

 Review: After reading

Read 1: Phonemic awareness

- Play 'find it!' by looking for the items in the small circles at the bottom of the pages, to build phonemic awareness. Choose an object or two per page and ask the children to find them in the photograph. Emphasise the initial sound of each word and then say the word. (e.g. Can you find a ppp pen?)
- When they have found the object, ask the children to say the first sound of the word.
- Look at pages 14 and 15 together and ask the children to describe some of the different people you find in a hospital, and why they are there.

Read 2: Vocabulary

- Encourage the children to hold the book and turn the pages.
- Spend time looking at the pictures and discussing them, drawing on any relevant experience or knowledge the children have. Encourage them to talk about what they can see in each picture, giving as much detail as they can. Expand the children's vocabulary by naming objects in the photographs that they do not know.
- Sound-talk a familiar object or two on each page (e.g. Can you find the t-oy? Can you find the m-a-n?) Sound-talk but do not blend the word. When the children find the object, encourage them to blend the word.

Read 3: Comprehension

- Read the book again. Ask:
  - What different things happen in a hospital? (e.g. *a doctor asks questions, visitors chat to patients, doctors examine children*)
  - What sort of tools, instruments or machines might you see in a hospital? (e.g. *clipboard, stethoscope, scanner, X-ray machine*)